THE GREAT LITTLE BOOK OF NOODLE DISHES

noodle know-how

THE GREAT LITTLE BOOK OF NOODLE DISHES

noodle know-how

emma summer

southwater

This edition is published by Southwater

Southwater is an imprint of Anness Publishing Ltd

Hermes House, 88–89 Blackfriars Road, London SE1 8HA
tel. 020 7401 2077; fax 020 7633 9499
www.southwaterbooks.com; info@anness.com

© Anness Publishing Ltd 1998, 2004

UK agent: The Manning Partnership Ltd,
6 The Old Dairy, Melcombe Road, Bath BA2 3LR;
tel. 01225 478444; fax 01225 478440; sales@manning-partnership.co.uk

UK distributor: Grantham Book Services Ltd,
Isaac Newton Way, Alma Park Industrial Estate, Grantham, Lincs NG31 9SD;
tel. 01476 541080; fax 01476 541061; orders@gbs.tbs-ltd.co.uk

North American agent/distributor: National Book Network,
4501 Forbes Boulevard, Suite 200, Lanham, MD 20706;
tel. 301 459 3366; fax 301 429 5746; www.nbnbooks.com

Australian agent/distributor: Pan Macmillan Australia,
Level 18, St Martins Tower, 31 Market St, Sydney, NSW 2000;
tel. 1300 135 113; fax 1300 135 103; customer.service@macmillan.com.au

New Zealand agent/distributor: David Bateman Ltd,
30 Tarndale Grove, Off Bush Road, Albany, Auckland;
tel. (09) 415 7664; fax (09) 415 8892

A CIP catalogue record for this book is available from the British Library.

Publisher Joanna Lorenz
Senior Cookery Editor Linda Fraser
Assistant Editor Sarah Ainley
Copy Editor Jenni Fleetwood
Designers Patrick McLeavey & Jo Brewer
Illustrator Anna Koska
Photographers Edward Allwright, Michelle Garrett, Amanda Heywood, Thomas Odulate
Recipes Kit Chan, Shirley Gill, Liz Trigg,
Steven Wheeler

Previously published as *Noodle*

1 3 5 7 9 10 8 6 4 2

NOTES

Bracketed terms are intended for American readers.

For all recipes, quantities are given in both metric and imperial measures and, where
appropriate,
measures are also given in standard cups and spoons. Follow one set, but not a mixture,
because they are not interchangeable.

Standard spoon and cup measures are level.

1 tsp = 5ml, 1 tbsp = 15ml, 1 cup = 250ml/8fl oz

Australian standard tablespoons are 20ml. Australian readers should use 3 tsp in place of 1
tbsp for measuring small quantities of gelatine, flour, salt, etc.

Medium (US large) eggs are used unless otherwise stated.

Contents

Introduction

Simple, speedy and satisfying, noodles are the original fast food. Their history goes back thousands of years, to the time when man first learned to grind grain. After the discovery that flour could be used to bake bread, it was a short step to finding that when it was mixed with water and pressed or rolled into thin sheets, it could be dried and kept for cooking at a later date.

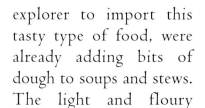

Long before Marco Polo made his much-vaunted voyages to the Far East, returning with recipes for ravioli and other specialities now almost exclusively associated with Italy, the art of noodle-making had been perfected in India, Japan, China, Malaysia and present-day Thailand. European cooks, far from sitting back waiting for an enterprising explorer to import this tasty type of food, were already adding bits of dough to soups and stews. The light and floury dumplings that resulted were known as "nudeln", which gave us the word that has become so familiar today.

Oriental noodles are made from a wide variety of grains, including buckwheat and rice, and are often enriched with egg. They may also be of vegetable origin. Cellophane noodles are made from mung beans, and soy beans, chick-peas, corn and even seaweed are just some of the sources of the hundreds of different varieties now available.

Noodle shops or restaurants are a familiar part of the street scene in many oriental cities. In Bangkok, noodle kiosks cater to city workers' insatiable appetites, while the *klongs* (canals) are thronged with noodle barges. Noodle sellers visit the suburbs, too, trundling their wares on trolleys from house to house. The situation is similar in Vietnam and Korea, while in Japan there are elegant specialist restaurants offering steaming bowls of noodle soup, simply prepared noodles with dipping sauces, and crystal-clear chilled noodle salads featuring beautifully carved vegetables. In many of these restaurants the noodle maker can be seen at work. Unlike his Italian counterpart, he does not roll and cut the dough, but shapes it to a short rope before twisting and whirling it through the air repeatedly to produce the long and slender strands.

As snacks and starters, noodles (and dishes made from noodle dough, such as filled wonton wrappers) really come into their own. Spring rolls must be one of the world's most convenient finger foods, and provide the perfect way of using up small quantities of meat, fish or vegetables. Fried plain wonton wrappers make delicious crisps in which to sandwich simple stir-fried mixtures. Noodle soups are popular the world over, and can be light and delicately flavoured or hearty main courses, with the stock serving merely to moisten the dish.

For both everyday family meals and entertaining, noodles are an excellent choice. Some types do not even need to be cooked, but are simply added to a pan of boiling water and left to stand while the cook swiftly stir-fries some crisp vegetables, and adds a savoury sauce. Noodles provide the ideal opportunity to become familiar with superb oriental ingredients like lemon grass and tamarind, and to discover a wonderful world of flavour – fast!

Ingredients

CELLOPHANE NOODLES

Sometimes sold as transparent, or glass, noodles, these are clear and shiny. They are generally made from mung bean flour and must be soaked in hot water before cooking. Unlike some oriental noodles, cellophane noodles can be reheated successfully after cooking, and are a favourite ingredient for stir-fries.

RICE NOODLES

Made from rice flour and water, these long dried noodle strands come in various thicknesses, ranging from very thin to wide ribbons and sheets, and are usually sold in neat bundles, tied with raffia. Fresh rice noodles are also available. Rinse rice noodles in warm water and drain before use. Rice noodles are traditionally served at Chinese birthday celebrations; the longer the strands, the more auspicious the omens for a long and healthy life.

EGG NOODLES

Available in skeins or bundles, egg noodles are widely used throughout Asia, and range from very thin strands to narrow ribbons. Both fresh and dried noodles are available, although the latter type is easier to come by. Egg noodles need little cooking: some varieties are simply added to boiling water; others need to be boiled briefly. Always follow the instructions on the packet.

RICE SHEETS

Square or round pieces of rice flour dough, these are used in much the same way as wonton wrappers, to provide a casing for a savoury filling. The sheets are naturally stiff and must be softened before being rolled, either by brushing them with hot water, or by dipping them briefly in hot water.

RICE STICKS

The name is somewhat misleading; rice sticks are simply flat, ribbon-like rice noodles, sold in skeins. As with other rice noodles, they must be soaked in hot water and drained before use.

RICE VERMICELLI

Thin, white and brittle, rice vermicelli is sold in large bundles. When pre-soaked and drained, it cooks almost instantly in hot liquid. Small quantities can also be deep-fried straight from the packet to make a crisp garnish for a soup or a sauce dish.

SOBA

These Japanese noodles are made from buckwheat (or a mixture of buckwheat and wheat flour) and are traditionally cooked in simmering water. Flavoursome and quite chewy, they may be served either hot or cold, with a dipping sauce.

SOMEN

Wheat flour is used to make these delicate white noodles. Like vermicelli, they cook very quickly in boiling water. Somen noodles are sold in dried form, usually tied in bundles that are held together with a paper band.

UDON

Thick and starchy, these noodles are similar to Italian pasta, and can be substituted for linguine. Made from wheat flour and water, they are usually round in shape. A dried wholewheat version is available in some wholefood shops. Udon are also sold fresh, in chilled vacuum packs, or pre-cooked.

WONTON WRAPPERS

It is perfectly possible to make your own wonton dough, but it needs to be rolled wafer-thin and most cooks prefer to buy it as wonton wrappers – neat 7.5cm/3in squares, dusted with cornflour. The wrappers can be frozen for up to six months. They thaw rapidly, ready for filling and frying, steaming or boiling. Wonton wrappers can also be deep-fried, rather like crisps, or used to make spring rolls.

9

Techniques

STORING

Store dried noodles in the original packaging in airtight containers in a cool, dry place. They will stay fresh for many months. Fresh noodles (available from the chilled cabinets in oriental food stores) keep for several days in the fridge if sealed in the plastic bag in which they were bought. Check use-by dates. Fresh egg noodles and wonton wrappers can be frozen successfully.

PREPARATION

Some noodles, notably cellophane noodles and rice noodles, must be soaked in hot water and drained before use. Follow the instructions in individual recipes. Noodles which are to be cooked twice (parboiled, then stir-fried or simmered in sauce) are initially cooked until they are barely tender, then drained, refreshed under cold running water, and drained again.

If appropriate, they may be tossed with a little oil to prevent any strands from sticking together. At this stage they can be stored in an airtight container in the fridge for several days.

COOKING

Add noodles to a large saucepan of rapidly boiling, lightly salted water, and cook for the time recommended on the packet. Unlike Italian pasta, which should retain a bit of bite, oriental noodles are cooked until they are tender. Avoid overcooking, however, which can make them soggy. Dried noodles are sometimes deep-fried for garnishing or for use as a noodle cake. In this case, do not pre-cook.

Preparing Additional Ingredients

MAKING TAMARIND WATER

Tamarind, the fruit of a tropical tree, is highly valued for its acidic flavour. Sold dry or as pulp, the fruit must be soaked in hot water before use. Mix about 15ml/1 tbsp pulp with 60ml/4 tbsp hot water in a bowl. Leave for 10 minutes, then strain into a clean bowl, pressing the pulp against the sieve to make a thick liquid (tamarind water). Use sparingly.

MAKING COCONUT MILK

To make 250ml/8fl oz/1 cup thick coconut milk (coconut cream), break 115g/4oz/$\frac{1}{2}$ cup creamed coconut into chunks and place it in a heatproof bowl. Stir in 150ml/$\frac{1}{4}$ pint/$\frac{2}{3}$ cup boiling water until the coconut is smooth and creamy. If the recipe calls for thin milk, soak 115g/4oz/$\frac{1}{2}$ cup creamed coconut in 250ml/8floz/1 cup boiling water in a

blender or food processor for 10 minutes. Process until smooth, then strain before use.

PREPARING LEMON GRASS

Cut off and discard the dry leafy tops, leaving about 15cm/6in of stalk. Peel away any tough outer layers, then lay the lemon grass on a board and bruise it with the flat blade of a cleaver or cook's knife. Cut the lemon grass into thin slices, or chop it finely.

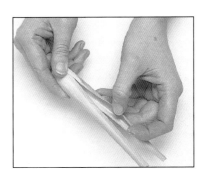

Snacks & Light Suppers

Spring Rolls

INGREDIENTS

6 Chinese dried mushrooms, soaked in hot
water for 30 minutes
225g/8oz/1 cup lean minced pork
115g/4oz raw prawns, peeled, deveined and
chopped
115g/4oz white crabmeat, picked over
1 carrot, shredded
50g/2oz cellophane noodles, soaked in
hot water until soft
4 spring onions, finely sliced
2 garlic cloves, finely chopped
30ml/2 tbsp fish sauce
juice of 1 lime
25 x 10cm/4in rice sheets
oil for deep-frying
ground black pepper
lettuce leaves, cucumber slices and
fresh coriander leaves, to garnish

MAKES 25

1 Drain the mushrooms and squeeze dry. Remove the stems and slice the caps thinly into a bowl. Add the pork, seafood and carrot. Drain the noodles, snip them into short lengths and add to the bowl with the spring onions and garlic. Stir in the fish sauce and lime juice. Season with pepper and set aside for 30 minutes to allow the flavours to blend.

2 Dip a rice sheet in a bowl of hot water to make it pliable, then lay it on a flat surface. Place about 5cm/2in of the filling near the edge of the rice sheet, fold both ends over, then roll up, sealing the roll with a little water.

3 Heat the oil to 180°C/350°F or until a cube of dried bread browns in 30–45 seconds. Add the rolls a few at a time and fry until golden brown and crisp. Drain  on kitchen paper and serve garnished with lettuce, cucumber and fresh coriander.

13

Rice Vermicelli & Salad Rolls

INGREDIENTS

*50g/ 2oz rice vermicelli, soaked in hot water
until soft and drained
1 large carrot, shredded
15ml/ 1 tbsp granulated sugar
15–30ml/ 1–2 tbsp fish sauce
8 x 20cm/ 8in round rice sheets
8 large lettuce leaves, trimmed
350g/ 12oz/ 6 cups Chinese roast pork, sliced
115g/ 4oz/ 2 cups beansprouts
handful of fresh mint leaves
8 cooked king prawns, peeled, deveined
and halved
½ cucumber, cut into fine strips
fresh coriander leaves*

PEANUT SAUCE

*15ml/ 1 tbsp vegetable oil
3 garlic cloves, finely chopped
1–2 fresh red chillies, finely chopped
5ml/ 1 tsp tomato purée
120ml/ 4fl oz/ ½ cup water
15ml/ 1 tbsp smooth peanut butter
30ml/ 2 tbsp hoisin sauce
2.5ml/ ½ tsp granulated sugar
juice of 1 lime
50g/ 2oz/ ½ cup peanuts, ground*

MAKES 8

1 Bring a saucepan of lightly salted water to the boil and cook the vermicelli for 2–3 minutes. Drain, rinse under cold water and drain again. In a bowl, mix the noodles, carrot, sugar and fish sauce.

2 Assemble the rolls one at a time. Dip a rice sheet in a bowl of hot water, then lay it flat. Place a lettuce leaf, 1–2 scoops of the noodle mixture, a few slices of pork, some of the beansprouts and several mint leaves on the rice sheet.

3 Start rolling the rice sheet into a cylinder. When half the sheet has been rolled, fold both sides towards the centre and lay 2 pieces of prawn along the crease. Add a few cucumber strips and coriander leaves, then finish rolling the sheet to make a tight packet. Place on a plate and cover with a damp dish towel while you make the remaining rolls.

4 Make the peanut sauce. Heat the oil in a small saucepan and fry the garlic and chillies for 1 minute. Add the tomato purée and the water and bring to the boil, then stir in the peanut butter, hoisin sauce, sugar and lime juice. Lower the heat and simmer for 3–4 minutes. Spoon the sauce into a bowl, add the ground peanuts and leave to cool.

5 To serve, cut each roll in half widthways to reveal the filling. Arrange on individual plates and add a spoonful of the peanut sauce to each. Garnish with any remaining coriander leaves and beansprouts.

Wonton Crisps with Seared Scallops

INGREDIENTS

16 scallops, halved
oil for deep-frying
8 wonton wrappers
45ml/3 tbsp olive oil
1 large carrot, cut into long thin strips
1 large leek, cut into long thin strips
juice of 1 lemon
juice of ½ orange
2 spring onions, finely sliced
30ml/2 tbsp fresh coriander leaves
salt and ground black pepper
MARINADE
5ml/1 tsp Thai red curry paste
5ml/1 tsp grated fresh root ginger
1 garlic clove, finely chopped
15ml/1 tbsp soy sauce
15ml/1 tbsp olive oil

SERVES 4

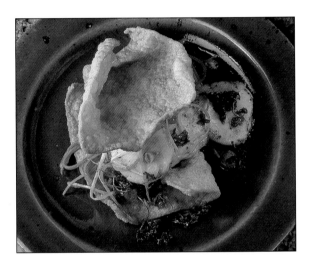

1 Make the marinade by mixing all the ingredients in a bowl. Add the scallops, toss to coat, then cover and marinate for 30 minutes. Meanwhile, heat the oil in a large heavy-based saucepan. Deep-fry the wonton wrappers in small batches until crisp and golden. Drain on kitchen paper and set aside.

2 Heat half the olive oil in a large frying pan. Add the scallops, with the marinade, and sear over a high heat for about 1 minute, until golden and just firm to the touch. Using a slotted spoon, transfer the scallops to a plate.

3 Add the remaining olive oil to the pan. When hot, stir-fry the carrot and leek strips until crisp-tender. Season with salt and pepper and stir in the citrus juices.

4 Return the scallops to the pan, mix lightly and warm through. Transfer to a bowl and add the spring onions and fresh coriander. Sandwich a quarter of the mixture between each pair of wonton crisps. Serve at once.

16

Chilli Squid with Noodles

INGREDIENTS

675g/ 1 ½lb fresh squid
30ml/ 2 tbsp vegetable oil
3 slices of fresh root ginger, peeled and finely shredded
2 garlic cloves, finely chopped
1 red onion, finely sliced
1 carrot, finely sliced
1 celery stick, sliced diagonally
50g/ 2oz sugar snap peas, topped and tailed
5ml/ 1 tsp granulated sugar
15ml/ 1 tbsp chilli bean paste
2.5ml/ ½ tsp chilli powder
75g/ 3oz cellophane noodles, soaked in hot water until soft
120ml/ 4fl oz/ ½ cup chicken stock
15ml/ 1 tbsp soy sauce
15ml/ 1 tbsp oyster sauce
5ml/ 1 tsp sesame oil
salt and ground black pepper
fresh coriander, to garnish

SERVES 4

1 Gently pull the squid's head and tentacles from its body. Discard the head; trim and reserve the tentacles. Remove the "quill" from inside the body and peel off the skin. Rub salt into the squid and wash in cold water. Cut the body into rings or squares.

2 Heat the oil in a flameproof casserole. Add the ginger, garlic and onion. Stir-fry for 1–2 minutes, then add the squid, carrot, celery and sugar snap peas. Stir-fry until the squid curls up. Stir in the sugar, chilli bean paste and chilli powder. Transfer the mixture to a bowl and set aside.

3 Drain the noodles. Combine the stock and sauces in the clean casserole. Bring to the boil, add the noodles and cook until tender. Add the squid mixture, cover and cook for 5–6 minutes more, until all the flavours are combined. Season to taste.

4 Serve on heated individual plates. Drizzle sesame oil over each portion and sprinkle with coriander.

Sweet & Sour Wonton Wrappers

INGREDIENTS

16–20 wonton wrappers
oil for deep-frying
SAUCE
15ml/1 tbsp vegetable oil
30ml/2 tbsp soft light brown sugar
45ml/3 tbsp rice vinegar
15ml/1 tbsp light soy sauce
15ml/1 tbsp tomato ketchup
45–60ml/3–4 tbsp chicken stock
15ml/1 tbsp cornflour, mixed to a paste with
a little water

SERVES 4

1 Make the sauce. Heat the oil in a wok or saucepan. Stir in the sugar, rice vinegar, soy sauce, ketchup and stock. Bring to the boil, then add the cornflour  paste, stirring constantly until the sauce is smooth and thick. Lower the heat so that the sauce barely simmers while you cook the wontons.

2 Pinch the centre of each wonton wrapper and twist it around to make the shape of a flower. Heat the oil in a wok or deep-fryer and fry the wonton wrap-  pers for 1–2 minutes, until crisp. Remove with a slotted spoon and drain on kitchen paper.

3 Divide the deep-fried wontons between four plates and spoon a little sauce over each portion. Serve at once, with extra sauce on the side.

Fried Cellophane Noodles

INGREDIENTS

*175g/6oz cellophane noodles, soaked in hot
water until soft*
45ml/3 tbsp vegetable oil
3 garlic cloves, finely chopped
115g/4oz cooked prawns, peeled and deveined
*2 lap cheong or other spicy dried sausages,
rinsed, drained and finely diced*
2 eggs
2 celery sticks, including leaves, diced
115g/4oz/2 cups beansprouts
115g/4oz spinach leaves, torn into large pieces
2 spring onions, chopped
15–30ml/1–2 tbsp fish sauce
5ml/1 tsp sesame oil
15ml/1 tbsp toasted sesame seeds, to garnish

SERVES 4

1 Drain the noodles, cut them into short lengths
and set aside. Heat the vegetable oil in a wok,
add the chopped garlic and fry until golden brown.
Add the prawns and lap cheong or other diced
sausage; stir-fry for 2–3 minutes. Stir in the
noodles and fry for 2 minutes more.

2 Make a well in
the centre of the
prawn mixture,
then break in the
eggs and stir them
gently over a low
heat until they
are creamy and
just set.

3 Add the celery, beansprouts, spinach and spring
onions to the wok. Season with fish sauce and
add the sesame oil. Toss over the heat until all the
ingredients are crisp-tender, then transfer to a
serving dish, sprinkle with sesame seeds and serve.

Egg Noodles in Soup

INGREDIENTS

225g/8oz skinless, boneless chicken breast
or pork fillet
3–4 Chinese dried mushrooms, soaked in hot
water for 30 minutes
115g/4oz canned sliced bamboo
shoots, drained
115g/4oz young spinach leaves
600ml/1 pint/2½ cups chicken stock
350g/12oz dried egg noodles
30ml/2 tbsp vegetable oil
2 spring onions, thinly sliced
5ml/1 tsp salt
2.5ml/½ tsp soft light brown sugar
15ml/1 tbsp soy sauce
10ml/2 tsp rice wine or dry sherry
few drops of sesame oil

SERVES 4

1 Using a cleaver or sharp knife, shred the meat finely. (If you put the meat in the freezer for 30 minutes before preparing it, it will be much easier to shred.) Drain the mushrooms and squeeze dry. Remove the stems and slice the caps thinly into a bowl. Shred the bamboo shoots and spinach leaves and add them to the bowl.

2 Bring the stock to the boil in a wok or saucepan. Fill a second pan with lightly salted water, bring it to the boil, then cook the egg noodles according to the instructions on the packet. Drain, rinse under cold water and drain again. Tip into a large serving bowl and pour over the hot stock. Keep the mixture hot.

3 Heat a wok and add the oil. When it is hot, stir-fry the chicken or pork with half the spring onions for 1 minute. Add the mushroom mixture and stir-fry for 2 minutes more or until the meat is cooked.

4 Stir the salt, brown sugar and soy sauce into the wok, with the rice wine or sherry. Toss to mix, heat through for about 30 seconds, then drizzle with the sesame oil.

5 Add the stir-fried mixture to the noodle soup, garnish with the remaining spring onions and serve.

Malay-Style Soupy Noodles

INGREDIENTS

15ml/ 1 tbsp vegetable oil
2 garlic cloves, very finely chopped
2 shallots, chopped
900ml/ 1½ pints/ 3¾ cups
chicken stock
225g/ 8oz lean beef or pork, thinly sliced
150g/ 5oz fish balls
4 raw king prawns, peeled and deveined
350g/ 12oz egg noodles
115g/ 4oz watercress
salt and freshly ground black pepper
GARNISH
115g/ 4oz/ 2 cups beansprouts
2 spring onions, sliced
15ml/ 1 tbsp fresh coriander leaves
2 red chillies, seeded and chopped
30ml/ 2 tbsp deep-fried onions

SERVES 4

1 Heat the oil in a large saucepan and fry the chopped garlic and shallots for 1 minute, then stir in the stock. Bring to the boil, then reduce the heat. Add the beef or pork, fish balls and prawns and simmer for 2 minutes.

2 Bring a large saucepan of water to the boil, add the noodles and cook until tender. Drain them well and divide among individual serving bowls.

3 Season the soup with salt and pepper, then add the watercress. The hot soup will cook it instantly.

4 Using a slotted spoon, scoop out the beef or pork, fish balls, prawns and the watercress from the soup and arrange them over the noodles.

Pour the hot soup over the top. Serve at once, sprinkled with each of the garnishing ingredients.

22

Spicy Shrimp & Noodle Soup

INGREDIENTS

150g/ 5oz dried rice noodles, soaked in hot
water until soft
25g/ 1oz/ ¼ cup raw cashew nuts
5cm/ 2in piece of lemon grass, shredded
2 garlic cloves, crushed
1 onion, finely chopped
30ml/ 2 tbsp vegetable oil
15ml/ 1 tbsp fish sauce
15ml/ 1 tbsp mild curry paste
400g/ 14oz can coconut milk
½ chicken stock cube
450g/ 1lb white fish fillets, skinned and cut
into bite-size pieces
225g/ 8oz raw prawns, peeled and deveined
1 small cos lettuce, shredded
115g/ 4oz/ 2 cups beansprouts
3 spring onions, shredded
½ cucumber, cut into matchsticks
shrimp crackers, to serve

SERVES 4–6

1 Bring a saucepan of lightly salted water to the boil. Add the noodles and cook according to the instructions on the packet. Drain, rinse under cold water and drain again. Using a mortar and pestle, or a food processor, grind the cashew nuts to a paste with the lemon grass, garlic and onion.

2 Heat the oil in a large wok or saucepan, add the nut paste and fry for 1–2 minutes, until the paste begins to brown.

3 Stir in the fish sauce, curry paste and coconut milk. Crumble in the stock cube. Simmer for 10 minutes, then place the fish and prawns in a large frying basket, immerse in the simmering liquid and cook for 3–4 minutes.

4 Line a large platter with the shredded lettuce. Arrange the beansprouts, spring onions, cucumber, fish, prawns, noodles and shrimp crackers in separate piles on top. Ladle the soup into bowls and invite guests to add their own accompaniments.

Noodles with Ginger

INGREDIENTS

handful of fresh coriander sprigs
225g/8oz dried egg noodles
45ml/3 tbsp groundnut oil
5cm/2in piece of fresh root ginger, peeled
and cut into fine shreds
6–8 spring onions, cut into shreds
30ml/2 tbsp light soy sauce
salt and ground black pepper

SERVES 4

24

1 Strip the leaves from the coriander stalks. Pile the leaves on a chopping board and chop them quite coarsely with a cleaver or sharp kitchen knife.

2 Cook the noodles according to the instructions on the packet. Drain, rinse under cold water and drain again. Tip into a bowl and toss with 15ml/1 tbsp of the oil.

3 Heat a wok, add the remaining oil and swirl it around. Stir-fry the ginger for a few seconds, then add the noodles and spring onions. Stir-fry for 3–4 minutes, until the spring onions are crisp-tender and the noodles are heated through.

4 Sprinkle the soy sauce and chopped fresh coriander over the noodles. Add salt and pepper to taste and toss over the heat for about 30 seconds more. Serve at once.

Chicken, Vermicelli & Egg Shred Soup

INGREDIENTS

3 large eggs
30ml/2 tbsp chopped fresh coriander
1.5 litres/2½ pints/6¼ cups chicken stock
115g/4oz vermicelli, broken into short lengths
115g/4oz cooked chicken, sliced
salt and ground black pepper

SERVES 4–6

1 Whisk the eggs in a small bowl and stir in the chopped coriander. Heat a small non-stick frying pan and pour in 30–45ml/ 2–3 tbsp of the mixture, swirling

to cover the bottom of the pan. Cook until set, then slide the omelette on to a board. Repeat until all the egg mixture is used up. Roll each omelette up. Using a sharp knife, slice thinly into shreds and set aside.

2 Bring the stock to the boil in a large saucepan. Add the vermicelli. Cook for 3–5 minutes, until almost tender, then add the chicken. Season with salt and black

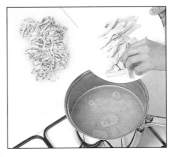

pepper and cook for 2–3 minutes, until the chicken is heated through.

3 Stir in the egg shreds and serve immediately, in heated individual bowls.

Stir-fried Noodles with Spinach

INGREDIENTS

15ml/1 tbsp sunflower oil
2.5cm/1in piece of fresh root ginger, grated
2 garlic cloves, crushed
45ml/3 tbsp dark soy sauce
150ml/¼ pint/⅔ cup boiling water
225g/8oz/2 cups peas, thawed if frozen
450g/1lb dried rice noodles
450g/1lb spinach leaves, coarse stalks removed
30ml/2 tbsp smooth peanut butter
30ml/2 tbsp tahini
150ml/¼ pint/⅔ cup milk
1 ripe avocado
roasted peanuts and peeled, cooked prawns,
to garnish

SERVES 6

1 Heat a wok and add the oil. When the oil is hot, stir-fry the ginger and garlic for 30 seconds. Add 15ml/1 tbsp of the soy sauce, then stir in the boiling water.

2 Add the peas and noodles to the wok, cook for 3 minutes, then add the spinach leaves. Toss over the heat for 1–2 minutes more, until the spinach is wilted and the noodles are tender, then drain the mixture and keep it hot.

3 Wipe out the wok and add the peanut butter, tahini and milk. Stir in the remaining 30ml/2 tbsp soy sauce and mix well. Bring to the boil and simmer for 1 minute. Meanwhile, cut the avocado in half, remove the stone and peel and slice the flesh neatly.

4 Return the pea, noodle and spinach mixture to the wok, with the avocado slices. Toss gently to mix and heat through. Serve on individual plates, with some of the peanut and tahini sauce spooned over each portion. Garnish with roasted peanuts and peeled, cooked prawns.

26

Main Course Dishes

Fried Singapore Noodles

INGREDIENTS

175g/6oz dried rice noodles, soaked in hot
water until soft
60ml/4 tbsp vegetable oil
2.5ml/½ tsp salt
2.5ml/½ tsp sugar
10ml/2 tsp curry powder
75g/3oz cooked prawns, peeled and deveined
175g/6oz cold roast pork, cut into matchsticks
1 green pepper, seeded and chopped
into matchsticks
75g/3oz Thai fish cakes (optional)
10ml/2 tsp dark soy sauce

SERVES·4

1 Drain the noo-
dles. Pat them dry
with kitchen paper.
Heat a wok, then
add half the oil.
When hot, add the
noodles and salt.
Toss over the heat
for 2 minutes, then

use two slotted spoons to drain the noodles and
transfer them to a serving dish. Keep hot.

2 Gently heat the
remaining oil in
the wok. Stir in the
sugar and curry
powder and fry for
30 seconds. Add
the prawns, pork
and pepper. Stir-
fry for 1 minute.

3 Return the noodles to the wok and add the Thai
fish cakes, if you are using them. Stir-fry for
2 minutes more, until heated through. Stir in the
soy sauce and serve immediately.

Stir-fried Noodles with Salmon

INGREDIENTS

350g/12oz salmon fillet
3 garlic cloves
30ml/2 tbsp Japanese soy sauce (shoyu)
30ml/2 tbsp sake
60ml/4 tbsp mirin or sweet sherry
5ml/1 tsp soft light brown sugar
10ml/2 tsp grated fresh root ginger
30ml/2 tbsp groundnut oil
*225g/8oz dried egg noodles, cooked
and drained*
50g/2oz/1 cup alfalfa sprouts
*30ml/2 tbsp sesame seeds, lightly toasted,
to garnish*

SERVES 4

1 Slice the salmon thinly and spread the slices out in a large shallow dish. Crush 1 garlic clove and slice the remaining garlic thinly. Mix the soy sauce, sake, mirin

or sherry, sugar, ginger and crushed garlic in a jug. Pour the mixture over the salmon slices, cover and marinate for 30 minutes.

2 Carefully drain the salmon slices, reserving the marinade. Scrape any remaining pieces of ginger or garlic off the fish, then arrange the salmon slices in a single layer in a large ovenproof dish and set aside. Pre-heat the grill.

3 Heat a wok, add the oil and swirl it around. Cook the sliced garlic until it is golden brown, then add the cooked noodles and reserved marinade. Stir-fry for 3–4 minutes, until the marinade has reduced to a syrupy glaze that coats the noodles.

4 Meanwhile, cook the salmon slices under the hot grill for 2–3 minutes without turning. When the salmon is tender, toss the alfalfa sprouts with the noodle mixture and arrange on four individual heated plates. Top the noodle mixture with the salmon slices and sprinkle the toasted sesame seeds over the top. Serve at once.

Seafood Chow Mein

INGREDIENTS

75g/ 3oz squid, cleaned (see Chilli Squid
with Noodles)
½ egg white
15ml/ 1 tbsp cornflour, mixed to a
paste with water
75g/ 3oz raw prawns, peeled, deveined and
cut in half lengthways
3–4 fresh scallops, each cut into 3–4 slices
250g/ 9oz dried egg noodles
75–90ml/ 5–6 tbsp vegetable oil
50g/ 2oz mangetouts, trimmed
2.5ml/ ½ tsp salt
2.5ml/ ½ tsp soft light brown sugar
15ml/ 1 tbsp rice wine or dry sherry
30ml/ 2 tbsp soy sauce
2 spring onions, finely sliced
vegetable stock to moisten (optional)
few drops of sesame oil

SERVES 4

1 Open up the body of the squid and score the inner flesh in a criss-cross pattern. Cut it into tiny pieces, each about the size of a stamp. Add them to a bowl of boiling water and leave until all of them have curled up. Rinse under cold water and drain.

2 Whisk the egg white and cornflour paste in a bowl, add the prawns and scallops and stir to coat. Bring a saucepan of lightly salted water to the boil and cook the noodles. Drain, rinse under cold water and drain again. Tip into a bowl and toss with 15ml/1 tbsp of the oil.

3 Heat 30–45ml/2–3 tbsp oil in a wok. Stir-fry the mangetouts and seafood for 2 minutes. Add the salt, sugar and the wine or sherry, then stir in half the soy sauce. Add half the spring onions and moisten with a little stock if necessary. Toss over the heat for 1 minute, then remove and keep hot.

4 Heat the remaining oil in the wok. Stir-fry the noodles with the remaining soy sauce for 2–3 minutes. Place in a serving dish and mix in the seafood mixture. Garnish with the remaining spring onions and drizzle with the sesame oil. Serve hot or cold.

Chicken & Vermicelli Stir-fry

INGREDIENTS

120ml/ 4fl oz/ ½ cup vegetable oil
*225g/ 8oz dried rice vermicelli, broken into
short lengths*
*150g/ 5oz French beans, topped, tailed and cut
in half lengthways*
1 onion, finely chopped
*2 skinless, boneless chicken breasts, about
175g/ 6oz each, cut into strips*
5ml/ 1 tsp chilli powder
225g/ 8oz cooked prawns, peeled and deveined
45ml/ 3 tbsp dark soy sauce
45ml/ 3 tbsp white wine vinegar
10ml/ 2 tsp caster sugar
fresh coriander sprigs, to garnish

SERVES 4

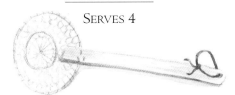

1 Heat a wok and add 60ml/4 tbsp of the oil. When hot, add the vermicelli in batches and fry until crisp. Remove with a slotted spoon and keep hot.

2 Heat the remaining oil in the wok, then add the French beans, onion and chicken. Stir-fry for about 3 minutes, until the chicken is cooked, then sprinkle in the chilli powder and toss over the heat for 1 minute more.

3 Add the prawns, soy sauce, white wine vinegar and caster sugar. Stir-fry for 2 minutes. Strew the fried vermicelli around the rims of four individual plates and pile a portion of the chicken mixture in the centre of each. Garnish with fresh coriander sprigs and serve at once.

33

Noodles with Spicy Meatballs

INGREDIENTS

350g/12oz dried egg noodles
45ml/3 tbsp sunflower oil
1 onion, thinly sliced
2 garlic cloves, crushed
5cm/1in piece of fresh root ginger, peeled and
cut into thin matchsticks
1.2 litres/2 pints/5 cups chicken stock
30ml/2 tbsp dark soy sauce
2 celery sticks, thinly sliced, leaves reserved
6 Chinese cabbage leaves, cut into
bite-size pieces
50g/2oz mangetouts, trimmed and cut
into strips
SPICY MEATBALLS
450g/1lb/2 cups minced beef
1 large onion, finely chopped
2 fresh red chillies, seeded and finely chopped
2 garlic cloves, crushed
15ml/1 tbsp ground coriander
5ml/1 tsp ground cumin
10ml/2 tsp dark soy sauce
5ml/1 tsp soft dark brown sugar
juice of 1/2 lemon
salt and ground black pepper
beaten egg, for binding
oil, for shallow frying

SERVES 6

1 Make the meatballs by putting all the ingredients in a large bowl and mixing thoroughly. Use only enough beaten egg to bind the mixture. Shape into small, evenly sized balls.

2 Bring a saucepan of lightly salted water to the boil and cook the noodles according to the instructions on the packet. Drain, rinse under cold water and drain again.

3 Heat the oil in a large shallow pan and fry the onion, garlic and ginger until softened. Pour in the stock and soy sauce and bring to the boil.

4 Add the meatballs to the pan, then lower the heat and simmer, partially covered, for 5 minutes. Add the celery slices, simmer for 2 minutes more, then add the Chinese cabbage and mangetouts. Simmer for 1 minute or until the meatballs are fully cooked.

5 Divide the noodles between six heated soup bowls. Add meatballs and vegetables to each bowl, then ladle stock on top. Garnish with the reserved celery leaves and serve.

34

Cellophane Noodles with Pork

INGREDIENTS

225g/8oz pork fillet, trimmed and cut into
very small cubes
30ml/2 tbsp dark soy sauce
30ml/2 tbsp rice wine or dry sherry
2 garlic cloves, crushed
15ml/1 tbsp grated fresh root ginger
5ml/1 tsp chilli oil
115g/4oz cellophane noodles, soaked in hot
water until soft
4 Chinese dried mushrooms, soaked in hot
water for 30 minutes
45ml/3 tbsp groundnut oil
4–6 spring onions, chopped
5ml/1 tsp cornflour, mixed with 175ml/
6fl oz/¾ cup chicken stock
30ml/2 tbsp chopped fresh coriander
salt and ground black pepper, to taste
fresh coriander sprigs, to garnish

SERVES 3–4

1 Put the pork in a bowl with the soy sauce, rice wine or sherry, garlic, ginger and chilli oil. Mix well, then cover and marinate for about 15 minutes.

2 Drain the noodles. Snip them into 13cm/5in lengths. Drain the mushrooms and squeeze dry. Remove the stems and chop the caps finely. Drain the pork, reserving the marinade.

3 Heat a wok and add the oil. When hot, stir-fry the pork and mushrooms for 3 minutes. Add the spring onions and toss over the heat for 1 minute more, then stir in the cornflour mixture with the reserved marinade. Cook for 1 minute, stirring.

4 Add the noodles and stir-fry for 2 minutes, until they have absorbed most of the liquid and the pork is cooked. Stir in the chopped fresh coriander, salt and pepper. Serve garnished with coriander sprigs.

Three-Meat Noodles

INGREDIENTS

450g/1lb dried egg noodles
1 skinless, boneless chicken breast
115g/4oz pork fillet, trimmed
115g/4oz lamb's liver
2 eggs
90ml/6 tbsp vegetable oil
25g/1oz/2 tbsp butter
2 garlic cloves, crushed
115g/4oz cooked prawns, peeled and deveined
115g/4oz young spinach leaves
2 celery sticks, thinly sliced
4 spring onions, finely chopped
60ml/4 tbsp chicken stock
dark soy sauce
salt and ground black pepper
deep-fried onions and celery leaves, to garnish

SERVES 6

37

1 Bring a saucepan of lightly salted water to the boil and cook the noodles. Drain, rinse under cold water and drain again.

2 Slice the chicken, pork and lamb's liver finely and set aside. Beat the eggs with salt and pepper to taste. Heat 5ml/1 tsp oil with the butter in a small frying pan. Stir in the eggs and cook over a low heat, stirring constantly until scrambled. Set aside.

3 Heat a wok, then add the remaining oil. Stir-fry the chicken, pork and liver with the garlic for 2–3 minutes, until the liver has changed colour. Add the prawns, spinach, celery and spring onions and toss over the heat for 2 minutes.

4 Add the drained noodles to the pan and toss again to mix. Moisten with the stock and add soy sauce to taste. Stir in the scrambled egg and serve, garnished with deep-fried onions and celery leaves.

Spicy Fried Rice Sticks

INGREDIENTS

15g/ ½oz dried shrimps, soaked in hot water
for 30 minutes
225g/ 8oz dried rice sticks, soaked in hot water
for 30 minutes
30ml/ 2 tbsp tamarind water
45ml/ 3 tbsp fish sauce
15ml/ 1 tbsp granulated sugar
2 garlic cloves, chopped
2 fresh red chillies, seeded and chopped
45ml/ 3 tbsp groundnut oil
2 eggs, beaten
225g/ 8oz cooked king prawns, peeled
and deveined
3 spring onions, cut into 2.5cm/ 1in lengths
75g/ 3oz/ 1½ cups beansprouts
30ml/ 2 tbsp chopped roasted unsalted peanuts
30ml/ 2 tbsp chopped fresh coriander
lime slices, to garnish

SERVES 4

1 Drain the shrimps and set them aside. Drain the rice sticks, rinse them under cold running water and drain again. Mix the tamarind water with the fish sauce and sugar.

2 Put the garlic and chillies in a mortar and use a pestle to pound them to a paste. Heat a wok, add 15ml/ 1 tbsp of the oil, then stir-fry the eggs over a medium heat until lightly scrambled. Transfer the eggs to a bowl and set aside. Wipe the wok clean.

3 Reheat the wok, add the remaining oil, then fry the chilli and garlic paste with the dried shrimps for 1 minute. Add the rice sticks and tamarind mixture; toss over the heat for 3–4 minutes.

4 Add the scrambled eggs, prawns, spring onions, beansprouts, peanuts and coriander to the wok. Toss over the heat for 2 minutes until heated through and well mixed. Serve at once on individual plates, garnishing each portion with lime slices.

COOK'S TIP

For a vegetarian dish, leave out the dried shrimps and use cubes of deep-fried, plain or smoked, firm tofu instead of the prawns.

Stir-fried Rice Noodles with Chicken & Prawns

INGREDIENTS

225g/ 8oz dried flat rice noodles, soaked in hot water until soft
120ml/ 4fl oz/ ½ cup water
60ml/ 4 tbsp fish sauce
15ml/ 1 tbsp granulated sugar
15ml/ 1 tbsp freshly squeezed lime juice
5ml/ 1 tsp paprika
pinch of cayenne pepper
45ml/ 3 tbsp vegetable oil
2 garlic cloves, crushed
1 skinless, boneless chicken breast, thinly sliced
8 raw prawns, peeled, deveined and cut in half lengthways
1 egg
50g/ 2oz/ ½ cup roasted peanuts, coarsely crushed
3 spring onions, cut into short lengths
175g/ 6oz/ 3 cups beansprouts
fresh coriander leaves and lime wedges, to garnish

SERVES 4

1 Drain the noodles, tip them into a bowl and set aside. Mix the water, fish sauce, sugar, lime juice, paprika and cayenne in a small bowl.

2 Heat a wok, add the oil, then fry the garlic for 30 seconds. Add the chicken slices and prawns and stir-fry for 3–4 minutes. Sweep the chicken mixture to the sides of the wok and add the egg to the centre. Cook the egg, stirring it constantly, until it is lightly scrambled.

3 Add the drained noodles and the fish sauce mixture to the wok. Mix well, then add half the crushed, roasted peanuts. Toss over the heat until the noodles are soft and most of the liquid has been absorbed.

4 Add the spring onions and two-thirds of the beansprouts to the wok. Toss over the heat for 1 minute more, then spoon on to a large serving platter and sprinkle with the remaining peanuts and beansprouts. Garnish with the fresh coriander and lime wedges and serve.

40

Noodles with Beef & Black Bean Sauce

INGREDIENTS

15ml/1 tbsp cornflour
30ml/2 tbsp soy sauce
30ml/2 tbsp oyster sauce
15ml/1 tbsp chilli black bean sauce
120ml/4fl oz/½ cup vegetable stock
60ml/4 tbsp vegetable oil
1 onion, thinly sliced
2 garlic cloves, crushed
2 slices of fresh root ginger, peeled and
finely chopped
225g/8oz mixed peppers, seeded and sliced
into strips
350g/12oz rump steak, finely sliced against
the grain
45ml/3 tbsp fermented black beans, rinsed in
hot water, drained and chopped
450g/1lb fresh rice noodles, rinsed in hot
water and drained
2 spring onions, finely chopped, and 2
fresh red chillies, seeded and finely sliced,
to garnish

SERVES 4

1 Put the cornflour in a small bowl. Stir in the soy sauce, oyster sauce and chilli black bean sauce, then add the stock and stir until smooth. Set aside.

2 Heat a wok and add half the oil. Stir-fry the onion, garlic, ginger and strips of mixed pepper for 3–5 minutes. Remove with a slotted spoon. Keep hot.

3 Heat the remaining oil in the wok. Stir-fry the steak with the fermented black beans over a high heat for 5 minutes. Return the stir-fried vegetables to the wok, add the cornflour mixture and cook, stirring, for 1 minute.

4 Add the noodles to the wok and toss over a medium heat until cooked. Taste, and add more soy sauce, if necessary. Tip the noodles into a heated bowl

and serve, garnished with the chopped spring onions and fresh chillies.

Vegetables & Salads

Tofu Noodles

INGREDIENTS

225g/8oz firm tofu
groundnut oil, for deep-frying
175g/6oz dried medium egg noodles
15ml/1 tbsp sesame oil
5ml/1 tsp cornflour
10ml/2 tsp dark soy sauce
30ml/2 tbsp rice wine or dry sherry
5ml/1 tsp granulated sugar
6–8 spring onions, cut diagonally
into 2.5cm/1in lengths
3 garlic cloves, sliced
1 fresh green chilli, seeded and sliced
115g/4oz Chinese cabbage leaves,
coarsely shredded
50g/2oz/1 cup beansprouts
50g/2oz/½ cup cashew nuts, toasted, to serve

SERVES 4

1 Drain the tofu, pat it dry with kitchen paper and cut into 2.5cm/1in cubes. Half-fill a wok with groundnut oil and heat it to 180°C/350°F or until a cube of dried bread added to the oil browns in 30–45 seconds. Deep-fry the tofu in batches for 1–2 minutes or until golden brown. Drain on kitchen paper. Carefully pour all but 30ml/2 tbsp of the oil from the wok.

2 Bring a saucepan of lightly salted water to the boil. Add the noodles and cook according to the instructions on the packet. Drain, rinse under cold water and drain again. Tip into a bowl and toss with 10ml/2 tsp of the sesame oil. Mix the cornflour, soy sauce, rice wine or sherry, sugar and remaining sesame oil in a small bowl.

3 Reheat the oil in the wok and stir-fry the spring onions, garlic, chilli, Chinese cabbage and beansprouts for 1–2 minutes. Toss in the tofu and noodles, then add the cornflour mixture. Cook, stirring, for 1 minute. Sprinkle with the toasted cashews and serve.

Crispy Noodles with Mixed Vegetables

INGREDIENTS

2 large carrots
2 courgettes
4 spring onions
115g/4oz fine green beans
115g/4oz dried rice vermicelli or
cellophane noodles
groundnut oil, for deep-frying
2.5cm/1in piece of fresh root ginger, peeled and
cut into shreds
1 fresh red chilli, sliced
115g/4oz/1 cup fresh shiitake or button
mushrooms, thickly sliced
a few Chinese cabbage leaves, coarsely shredded
75g/3oz/1½ cups beansprouts
30ml/2 tbsp light soy sauce
30ml/2 tbsp rice wine or dry sherry
5ml/1 tsp granulated sugar
30ml/2 tbsp torn fresh coriander leaves

SERVES 3–4

1 Cut the carrots, courgettes and spring onions into matchsticks. Trim the beans. Break the vermicelli or noodles into 7.5cm/3in lengths.

2 Half-fill a wok with groundnut oil and heat it to 180°C/350°F or until a cube of dried bread added to the oil browns in 30–45 seconds. Deep-fry the dried 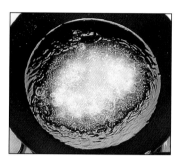 vermicelli or noodles, a handful at a time, for 1–2 minutes, until puffed up and crisp. Drain on kitchen paper. Carefully pour away all but 30ml/ 2 tbsp of the oil from the wok.

3 Reheat the oil in the wok and stir-fry the beans and carrots for 2–3 minutes. Add the ginger, chilli, mushrooms and courgettes and stir-fry for 1–2 minutes more.

4 Add the Chinese cabbage, bean-sprouts and spring onions and stir-fry for 1 minute more. Spoon over the soy sauce, rice wine or sherry and sugar. Toss over the heat  for 30 seconds, then add the vermicelli or noodles and the fresh coriander. Toss to mix, taking care not to crush the noodles, then serve.

46

Sesame Noodle Salad with Hot Peanuts

INGREDIENTS

350g/12oz dried egg noodles
2 carrots, cut into matchsticks
½ cucumber, peeled and cubed
115g/4oz celeriac, cut into matchsticks
6 spring onions, finely sliced
8 canned water chestnuts, drained and
finely sliced
175g/6oz/3 cups beansprouts
1 fresh green chilli, seeded and finely chopped
30ml/2 tbsp sesame seeds and
115g/4oz peanuts, to serve
DRESSING
15ml/1 tbsp dark soy sauce
15ml/1 tbsp light soy sauce
15ml/1 tbsp clear honey
15ml/1 tbsp rice wine or dry sherry
15ml/1 tbsp sesame oil

SERVES 4

1 Preheat the oven to 200°C/400°F/Gas 6. Bring a saucepan of lightly salted water to the boil. Add the noodles and cook according to the instructions on the packet. Drain the noodles, rinse under cold water and drain again.

2 Tip the noodles into a bowl and add the prepared vegetables, including the chilli. Mix well. Combine the dressing ingredients in a small bowl, whisk lightly, then add to the salad and toss to coat. Divide the salad between four plates.

3 Spread out the sesame seeds and peanuts on separate baking sheets. Bake the sesame seeds for 5 minutes and the peanuts for 10 minutes or until evenly browned.

4 Sprinkle the roasted seeds and peanuts over the four plates of salad and serve.

Stir-fried Vegetables with Ribbon Noodles

INGREDIENTS

450g/1lb dried ribbon noodles,
such as tagliatelle
45ml/3 tbsp corn oil
1cm/½in piece of fresh root ginger, peeled
and finely chopped
2 garlic cloves, crushed
1 carrot, sliced diagonally
2 courgettes, quartered lengthways,
then sliced diagonally
175g/6oz runner beans, sliced diagonally
175g/6oz baby corn cobs, halved lengthways
90ml/6 tbsp yellow bean sauce
6 spring onions, sliced into 2.5cm/1in lengths
30ml/2 tbsp rice wine or dry sherry
5ml/1 tsp sesame seeds
salt

SERVES 4

1 Bring a large saucepan of lightly salted water to the boil. Cook the ribbon noodles according to the instructions on the packet. Drain, rinse under hot water and drain again. Tip into a bowl and toss with 5ml/1 tsp of the oil.

2 Heat the rest of the oil in a wok or frying pan and stir-fry the ginger and garlic for 30 seconds, then add the vegetables. Stir-fry for 3–4 minutes.

3 Stir in the yellow bean sauce. Toss over the heat for 2 minutes, then add the spring onions, rice wine or sherry and drained ribbon noodles. Season with salt to taste.

Toss over the heat for 1 minute to heat through. Sprinkle with the sesame seeds and serve at once.

49

Noodles with Shiitake & Red Onion

INGREDIENTS

500g/ 1¼lb thin dried tagliarini
45ml/ 3 tbsp sesame oil
1 red onion, thinly sliced
115g/ 4oz fresh shiitake mushrooms, trimmed
and thinly sliced
45ml/ 3 tbsp dark soy sauce
15ml/ 1 tbsp balsamic vinegar
10ml/ 2 tsp caster sugar
5ml/ 1 tsp salt
celery leaves, to garnish

SERVES 6

3 Add the noodles to the wok, with the soy sauce, balsamic vinegar, caster sugar and salt. Stir-fry for 1 minute more, then add the remaining sesame oil. Toss

over the heat for 30 seconds. Garnish with celery leaves and serve at once.

1 Bring a large saucepan of lightly salted water to the boil. Add the noodles and cook according to the instructions on the packet. Drain, rinse under hot

water and drain again. Tip into a bowl and toss with 5ml/ 1 tsp of the oil.

2 Meanwhile, heat a wok, add 15ml/ 1 tbsp of the remaining oil and stir-fry the onion and shiitake mushrooms for 2 minutes.

Courgettes with Noodle Needles

Ingredients

450g/1lb courgettes
30ml/2 tbsp vegetable oil
1 onion, thinly sliced
1 garlic clove, crushed
2.5ml/½ tsp ground turmeric
2 tomatoes, chopped
45ml/3 tbsp water
400g/14oz cooked prawns, peeled and deveined
25g/1oz cellophane noodles
salt or soy sauce

Serves 4–6

1 Use a vegetable peeler to cut thin strips from the outside of each courgette. Cut the courgettes into thin slices. The slices will have decorative edges.

2 Heat the oil in a frying pan or wok and fry the onion and garlic for 5 minutes, until softened but not browned. Stir in the courgette slices and ground turmeric, then add the chopped tomatoes, water and prawns.

3 Put the noodles in a saucepan and pour over boiling water to cover. Leave for 1–2 minutes, then drain. Snip into 5cm/2in "needles" and add to the vegetables.

4 Cover with a lid and cook the noodles and vegetables in their own steam for 2–3 minutes. Toss well, season to taste with salt or soy sauce and serve at once.

51

Thai Noodle Salad

INGREDIENTS

350g/12oz dried somen noodles
1 large carrot, cut into thin strips
1 bunch asparagus, trimmed and cut into
4cm/1½in lengths
115g/4oz mangetouts, topped,
tailed and halved
115g/4oz baby corn cobs, halved lengthways
1 red pepper, seeded and cut into fine strips
115g/4oz/2 cups beansprouts
8 canned water chestnuts, drained and
thinly sliced
lime wedges, chopped roasted peanuts and
fresh coriander leaves, to garnish

DRESSING
45ml/3 tbsp torn fresh basil leaves
75ml/5 tbsp roughly chopped mint leaves
2 spring onions, thinly sliced
15ml/1 tbsp grated fresh root ginger
2 garlic cloves, crushed
250ml/8fl oz/1 cup coconut milk
30ml/2 tbsp dark sesame oil
juice of 1 lime
salt and cayenne pepper

SERVES 4–6

1 Make the dressing. Combine the fresh herb leaves and spring onions in a bowl. Add the ginger and garlic, coconut milk, sesame oil and lime juice. Whisk well, then season to taste with the salt and cayenne.

2 Bring a saucepan of lightly salted water to the boil. Add the noodles and cook according to the instructions on the packet. Drain, rinse under cold water and drain again.

3 Cook the carrot, asparagus, mangetouts and corn in separate saucepans of lightly salted boiling water until crisp-tender. Drain, refresh under cold water and drain again. Tip into a bowl and add the red pepper, beansprouts and water chestnuts.

4 Add the noodles and dressing to the bowl and toss well. Arrange on individual plates and garnish with the lime wedges, peanuts and coriander leaves.

Easy Entertaining

Pork Satay with Crisp Noodle Cake

INGREDIENTS

3 garlic cloves, crushed
15ml/1 tbsp Thai curry powder
5ml/1 tsp ground cumin
5ml/1 tsp granulated sugar
15ml/1 tbsp fish sauce
90ml/6 tbsp vegetable oil
450g/1lb lean pork, cut into 5cm/2in strips
350g/12 oz dried egg noodles, cooked, rinsed and drained
fresh coriander leaves, to garnish
SATAY SAUCE
30ml/2 tbsp vegetable oil
2 garlic cloves, finely chopped
1 small onion, finely chopped
2.5ml/½ tsp hot chilli powder
5ml/1 tsp Thai curry powder
250ml/8fl oz/1 cup coconut milk
15ml/1 tbsp fish sauce
30ml/2 tbsp granulated sugar
30ml/2 tbsp lemon juice
165g/5½oz/½ cup peanut butter

SERVES 4

I Mix the garlic, spices, sugar, fish sauce and 30ml/2 tbsp vegetable oil in a bowl. Add the meat, toss to coat, then cover and marinate for at least 2 hours. Soak eight bamboo skewers in cold water.

2 Make the satay sauce. Heat the oil in a heavy-based saucepan and fry the garlic and onion for 1 minute. Stir in the spices and fry for 2 minutes. Add the remaining ingredients. Mix well. Cook over a low heat for 20 minutes, stirring frequently, until the sauce thickens.

3 Heat 15ml/1 tbsp of the remaining oil in a large frying pan. Spread the noodles in the pan and fry for 4–5 minutes until crisp and golden. Turn the noodle cake over carefully and cook the other side. Keep hot. Preheat the grill or light the barbecue.

4 Drain the meat and thread it neatly on to the drained skewers. Cook over medium coals or under the grill for 8–10 minutes, turning occasionally and brushing the satays with oil. Transfer to a platter, garnish with fresh coriander and serve with wedges of noodle cake and the satay sauce.

55

Fruit & Vegetable Gado-Gado

INGREDIENTS

½ cucumber, sliced
2 pears, not too ripe
1–2 eating apples
30ml/2 tbsp lemon juice
1 small crisp lettuce, shredded
6 small tomatoes, cut into wedges
3 fresh pineapple slices, cored and
cut into wedges
12 hard-boiled quail's eggs, shelled
175g/6oz dried egg noodles, cooked, rinsed,
drained and cut into short lengths
salt
deep-fried onions, to garnish
PEANUT SAUCE
15ml/1 tbsp sambal oelek or chilli sauce
300ml/½ pint/1¼ cups coconut milk
350g/12oz/1 cup crunchy peanut butter
15ml/1 tbsp dark soy sauce
10ml/2 tsp thick tamarind water
15ml/1 tbsp peanuts, coarsely crushed
salt

SERVES 6

1 Put the cucumber slices in a colander and sprinkle them with salt. Leave in the sink for 15 minutes to drain, then rinse thoroughly and drain again.

2 Then make the peanut sauce. Mix the sambal oelek or chilli sauce with the coconut milk in a saucepan. Add the peanut butter and heat gently, stirring, until the sauce is smooth and thick. Stir in the soy sauce and tamarind water. Pour the sauce into a bowl and sprinkle with the crushed peanuts to serve.

3 Peel the pears and the apples, remove the cores and slice thinly into a bowl. Toss with the lemon juice. Arrange the fruit slices on a platter with the lettuce wedges, cucumber slices, tomatoes and pineapple wedges.

4 Arrange the quail's eggs over the salad and add the chopped noodles and deep-fried onions. Serve with the peanut sauce.

Lemon Grass Prawns

INGREDIENTS

300g/11oz thin dried egg noodles, cooked
and drained
60ml/4 tbsp vegetable oil
500g/1¼lb raw king prawns, peeled
and deveined
2.5ml/½ tsp ground coriander
15ml/1 tbsp ground turmeric
2 garlic cloves, finely chopped
2 slices of fresh root ginger, peeled and
finely chopped
2 lemon grass stalks, finely chopped
2 shallots, finely chopped
15ml/1 tbsp tomato purée
250ml/8fl oz/1 cup coconut cream
15–30ml/1–2 tbsp fresh lime juice
15–30ml/1–2 tbsp fish sauce
1 cucumber, peeled, seeded and cut into
5cm/2in batons
1 tomato, peeled, seeded and cut into strips
2 fresh red chillies, seeded and thinly sliced
salt and ground black pepper
spring onions and fresh coriander, to garnish

SERVES 4

1 Fry the noodles in 15ml/1 tbsp of the oil as described for Pork Satay with Crisp Noodle Cake (page 55), to make four individual cakes. Keep hot.

2 Put the prawns, ground spices, garlic, ginger and lemon grass in a bowl. Add salt and pepper to taste and toss to coat. Heat the remaining oil in a large frying pan and stir-fry the shallots for 1 minute, then add the seasoned prawns and stir-fry for 2 minutes. Remove the prawns with a slotted spoon.

3 Stir the tomato purée and coconut cream into the mixture remaining in the pan. Add lime juice and fish sauce to taste. Bring to simmering point, then add the cucumber. Return the prawns to the sauce and simmer for 3–4 minutes, until they are tender and the sauce is thick.

4 Add the tomato, stir until heated, then add the chillies. Serve on the noodle cakes, garnished with sliced spring onions and fresh coriander sprigs.

Noodle & Cabbage Rolls

INGREDIENTS

4 Chinese dried mushrooms, soaked in hot
water for 30 minutes
50g/ 2oz cellophane noodles, soaked in hot
water until soft and drained
450g/ 1lb/ 2 cups minced pork
4 spring onions, finely chopped
2 garlic cloves, finely chopped
30ml/ 2 tbsp fish sauce
12 large outer leaves of green cabbage
4 spring onions
30ml/ 2 tbsp vegetable oil
1 small onion, finely chopped
2 garlic cloves, crushed
400g/ 14oz can chopped tomatoes
pinch of granulated sugar
salt and ground black pepper

SERVES 4

1 Drain the mushrooms and squeeze dry. Remove the stems and chop the caps. Place them in a bowl. Snip the noodles into short lengths and add them to the bowl with the pork, spring onions and garlic. Season with the fish sauce and mix well.

2 Cut out the stem from each cabbage leaf. Bring a pan of water to the boil and blanch the leaves and whole spring onions for 1 minute. Refresh the vegetables under cold water and drain. Pat dry with kitchen paper. Split each spring onion into ribbons by cutting through the bulb and tearing upwards.

3 Place a spoonful of the pork filling in the centre of each cabbage leaf. Roll up the leaf to make a neat parcel. Tie each roll with a spring onion ribbon.

4 Heat the oil in a large frying pan and fry the onion and garlic over a low heat for 5 minutes. Stir in the tomatoes, with salt, pepper and sugar to taste. Heat gently, then add the cabbage parcels. Simmer, covered, for 20–25 minutes, or until the cabbage rolls are fully cooked. Serve hot.

Braised Birthday Noodles

INGREDIENTS

1kg/ 2¼lb lean neck fillet of lamb, cut into
5cm/ 2in thick medallions
30ml/ 2 tbsp vegetable oil
350g/ 12oz dried thick egg noodles
15ml/ 1 tbsp cornflour
30ml/ 2 tbsp soy sauce
15ml/ 1 tbsp hoisin sauce
30ml/ 2 tbsp rice wine or dry sherry
grated rind and juice of ½ orange
15ml/ 1 tbsp red wine vinegar
5ml/ 1 tsp soft light brown sugar
115g/ 4oz fine green beans, trimmed
and blanched
salt and ground black pepper
2 halved hard-boiled eggs and chopped spring
onions, to garnish
MARINADE
2 garlic cloves, crushed
10ml/ 2 tsp grated fresh root ginger
30ml/ 2 tbsp soy sauce
30ml/ 2 tbsp rice wine or dry sherry
1–2 dried red chillies
30ml/ 2 tbsp vegetable oil

SERVES 4

1 Mix together all the ingredients for the marinade in a large shallow dish. Add the lamb medallions, turn to coat, and marinate for at least 4 hours or overnight.

2 Heat the oil in a large heavy-based saucepan. Fry the lamb for 5 minutes, until it is browned, then add just enough water to cover. Bring to the boil, skim,  then lower the heat and simmer for 40 minutes or until tender, adding more water if necessary.

3 Bring a large saucepan of lightly salted water to the boil. Add the noodles and cook for 1 minute only. Drain, rinse under cold water and drain again. Set aside.

4 Mix the cornflour with the soy sauce and hoisin sauce, rice wine or sherry, orange rind and juice, vinegar and brown sugar. Add to the lamb and cook, stirring, until the sauce thickens.

5 Add the noodles and beans. Simmer, stirring occasionally, until both are fully cooked. Season and serve in individual bowls, garnished with the hard-boiled eggs and chopped spring onions.

Fragrant Chicken Curry with Vermicelli

INGREDIENTS

1 chicken, about 1.4–1.6kg/3–3½lb
225g/8oz sweet potatoes
60ml/4 tbsp vegetable oil
1 onion, thinly sliced
3 garlic cloves, crushed
30–45ml/2–3 tbsp Thai curry powder
5ml/1 tsp granulated sugar
10ml/2 tsp fish sauce
1 lemon grass stalk, cut in half
600ml/1 pint/2½ cups coconut milk
350g/12oz rice vermicelli, soaked in hot water until soft
lemon wedges, to serve
GARNISH
115g/4oz/2 cups beansprouts
2 spring onions, sliced diagonally
2 fresh red chillies, sliced diagonally
8–10 fresh mint leaves

SERVES 4

1 Skin the chicken. Cut the flesh into small pieces and set it aside. Peel the sweet potatoes and cut them into chunks, about the same size as the pieces of chicken.

2 Heat half the vegetable oil in a heavy-based saucepan and fry the onion and garlic over a low heat for 5 minutes. Push the onion and garlic to the side of the pan and stir-fry the chicken pieces until they change colour.

3 Stir in the curry powder, cook for 1 minute, then add the sugar, fish sauce and lemon grass. Pour in the coconut milk and cook over a low heat for about 15 minutes.

4 Meanwhile, heat the remaining oil in a large frying pan and fry the sweet potatoes until they turn pale gold. Using a slotted spoon, remove them from  the pan and add them to the chicken mixture. Cook for 15 minutes more, until both the chicken and the sweet potatoes are tender.

5 Drain the vermicelli. Bring a saucepan of lightly salted water to the boil and cook the vermicelli for 2–3 minutes, until tender. Drain, then divide between four individual shallow bowls and top with the chicken curry. Garnish with beansprouts, spring onions, chillies and mint leaves, and serve with lemon wedges.

Index